Spiritual Health

Book #3 in the Little Book Series

**Kent Philpott
Katie Philpott**

Spiritual Health

©2018 by Kent Philpott

All rights reserved.
Earthen Vessel Media, LLC
San Rafael, CA 94903
www.evpbooks.com

ISBN: 978-1-946794-10-9 print
ISBN: 978-1-946794-11-6 EPUB
Library of Congress Control Number: 2018960545

Cover and Interior design by KLC Philpott

The author and publisher hereby gives permission to quote, copy, or exerpt passages of any size from this book and requests it will be for the purposes of teaching and evangelism for the cause of Christ.

All Biblical Scripture quotations, unless otherwise indicated, are taken from the Holy Bible, English Standard Version® (ESV®), copyright © 2001 by Crossway Bibles, a publishing ministry of Good News Publishers. All rights reserved.

Contents

Preface	5
Love God and Love Your Neighbor	7
Confession is Good for You	14
Accepting Forgiveness	20
Growing into the Fullness of Christ	26
Having Meaning and Purpose	32
Keeping in Fellowship	39
Expect Opposition	46
End Times	53
Suffering Is to Be Expected	60
The Great Hope	66
Peace Beyond Understanding	73
The Best Sex	78
Being Alone	84
Anxiety and Worry	91
Sabbath Rest	96
Postscript	103

Preface

Looking back on the five decades I have been in Christian ministry, most of it as a pastor of congregations, I have noticed that faithful Christians, those who trust in Jesus Christ as Savior and Lord and who value the revealed Word of God, the Bible, tend to live well.

There are exceptions, of course—disease, calamity, and death come upon the most faithful. This harsh reality even tempts us to question the goodness of God.

I have had my share of deeply troubling life events. Then I have regrets over the consequences of my own sinful behavior. Still today, when I allow myself to dwell on the pain and suffering I have caused others, I become saddened, even depressed. Then comes the natural aging process; indeed, my body is wearing out, I have lost some mental acuity, and many things I formerly thought nothing of accomplishing are now beyond my ability.

Certainly, LIFE happens to us all. Misfortunes are not the result of any kind of punishment from God, but this side of heaven, things happen. This is made clear from the accounts of what happened to Moses, David, Jesus, Paul, and all the rest of those who appear in Scripture. Down through the history of the Church with its persecutions, we see Christians suffering.

It is amid the sufferings, whether light or serious, that the Christian's hope for this life and the next makes the difference. We all experience this "fallen world" as we journey on to forever being in the glorious presence of God in heaven. This "pilgrim's progress" is indeed progress.

I am now 76 years old, and by the time this 'Little Book' is published, I might be 77. Despite that, especially due to having pastored hundreds over the decades, I can say without exaggeration, that biblical Christianity is healthy.

As you read through my reasons for saying so, you may come across a topic I missed, which might result in a new chapter for a new edition.

    Email me at: kentphilpott@comcast.net.

Chapter One

Love God and Love Your Neighbor

When Jesus was asked about the greatest commandment in the Law, He replied:

> You shall love the Lord your God with all your heart and with all your soul and with all your mind. This is the great and first commandment. And a second is like it: You shall love your neighbor as yourself. On these two commandments depend all the Law and the Prophets. (Matthew 22:37–40)

Obeying the command to love God with the whole of us and honoring God above all else is healthy, because it keeps us from idol worship, and we tend to make idols out of almost anything or anyone. No idol can love us, guide us, save us, or be in fellowship with us. Idol worship leads to despair.

There is also the golden rule: "So whatever you wish that others would do to you, do also to them, for this is the Law and the Prophets"[1] (Matthew 7:12).

---

[1] "Law and the Prophets" is a common Jewish expression for all of the Hebrew Bible, or Old Testament.

"Love" for God means whole-hearted love, with no room for worship of or devotion to any other gods or goddesses. "Love" for the neighbor seeks the best for those whom we might encounter, not merely the folks next door. This "rule" is helpful, since we generally know how we ourselves would like to be treated.

The Parable of the Good Samaritan illustrates the point. Jesus tells the story of a Jewish man who is waylaid by robbers and beaten almost to death. A Samaritan finds the Jewish man, and at considerable time and expense he makes sure the traumatized man receives care and comfort, yet the Samaritans and Jews detested one another (see Luke 10:25–37).

How Is this Healthy?

A focus on ourselves is common to us all, and necessarily so. We must see to our own well-being and develop hope for the future. Here is where Jesus makes it clear that we are to "love" ourselves. This does not have to be a "me-first" mentality at all, but a reasonable and healthy injunction to care for ourselves.

It is not healthy to think of ourselves as bad people, although most of us do so from time to time. However, when we get stuck there and denigrate ourselves for whatever reasons, we need to see that this is not as it should be. It may indicate that we are suffering from something else, something that needs attention, perhaps even with the help of mental health professionals.

Sometimes we exhaust our own inner strength and turn to outside stimulation. Street drugs, alcohol, sexual excess, or frantic and risky behavior can spiral our lives downward. Trouble builds in every way—mentally, emotionally, physically, and spiritually.

We live in a world filled with high stress and anxiety; our world is complex and scary. Wars and threats of war, nation against nation, and trouble everywhere, at least our awareness of it via our connected world, is now the norm. Have humans evolved to the point where we can cope with the stress factors that swirl about us? Not yet, I think, and maybe never.

When our thoughts are constantly turned inward, anxiety only grows. And we soon discover there is little, if any, hope for the future. However 'deep' we attempt to go into our inner being, we will be disappointed when we find only emptiness or frightening images.

When we focus outwardly and go looking for love, it is often in all the wrong places, leaving us with a love that is fleeting and maybe not love at all. Loneliness grows, and hope recedes. Some cope, others do not. Some want to end it all; others lose contact with reality and experience psychotic states. This is real for many of us.

Again, it is not wrong to be concerned about ourselves, yet we are to love God with all of who we are. The focus shifts, not away from ourselves, but upward toward the God who created us and loves us. It is almost preposterous that the Triune God—Father, Son, and Holy Spirit—should love us who have rebelled against Him, but He does. "For God so loved the world, that he gave his only Son, that whoever believes in him should not perish but have eternal life" (John 3:16). And if that is not enough, there is this wonderful verse: "In this is love, not that we loved God but that he loved us and sent his son to be the propitiation for our sins" (1 John 4:10).

"Propitiation" is a theological term and means that Jesus, the Son, took all our sin, transgressions, rebellious ways, wrong doing, etc., upon Himself when He died on the cross. While this might not make much sense to us, it is nevertheless the truth.

"Love" in the passages above, both John 3:16 and 1 John 4:10, is transliterated from the Greek, *agape*. It means that God loves us and wants the very best for us, which is eternal fellowship with Him in heaven. Jesus literally died in our place. Only God could make this preposterous and absurd sacrifice, at least from our perspective, and all because of His love for us.

Sin is not good for us. Not only does it wreak havoc in our lives, it separates us from God forever. Yes, forever, and yes, I mean hell. Now hell is where God is not. Because God is holy, meaning that sin cannot ever come before Him, it means that if we die unforgiven, we cannot be in His presence, ever.

We have to admit no one knows why the Creator God has allowed all this to happen. What we do know is that it has happened, but that this same God has done something about it. This is the story of Jesus.

From our limited perspective we are unable to figure it all out. This is why we have the Bible, the written Word of God that reveals the Living Word of God, Jesus the Messiah. He died in our place because of love, real love, a love that does not go away.

Never Alone

Biblical Christianity is healthy, because it brings love to us. Jesus never leaves us; He continues to love us despite ourselves. This is what JOY is all about. Joy is not jumping around waving our arms in the air and shouting halleluiah, though some will do this; no, this joy is the recognition that we are loved with a love that will never fail. We have a Savior who will never turn away and never abandon us, despite how weird and strange we may be at times. Indeed, He wants us to be with Him forever. Jesus put it this way:

> Let not your hearts be troubled. Believe in God, believe also in me. In my Father's house are many rooms. If it were not so, would I have told you that I go to prepare a place for you, I will come again and will take you to myself, that where I am you may be also. (John 14:1–3)

Meaning and Purpose

There is another reason why biblical Christianity is healthy. Every Christian not only has meaning in his or her life, but we have been assigned a job to do, one from which no one retires, one that gives us MEANING. This is the commission Jesus gave us just before He ascended back to heaven.[2] Here it is, Matthew 28:19–20:

> Go therefore and make disciples of all nations, baptizing them in the name of the Father and of the Son and of the Holy Spirit, teaching them to observe all that I have commanded you. And behold, I am with you always, to the end of the age.

It cannot get any better than this. Let me make it plain: it is not an easy road to travel and is the road less travelled, but there is no better way. It never gets boring, we are never alone, the adventure never dies down, and there is no retirement age.

HOPE does not fade either. Bible hope is not a wish, it is a sure thing. I do not have the words to express what I mean here. The common understanding of the word hope does not begin to define the biblical meaning of the term. My hope is in Jesus Christ and what He

---

[2] Heaven is the dwelling place of God. It is not in the physical universe; in fact, we know little about it, but one day we will know all about it.

has already done for me. It is a done deal. As Jesus said while hanging of the cross, "It is finished." Nothing can change that, not even stupid and sinful things that I do. No, I do not have a license to sin, but an hour hardly goes by that I do not sin in some manner or other. After all, we are to love God with all we are and have and also to love our neighbor as ourselves. Who can say they meet this challenge? My hope, my assurance has nothing to do with my spirituality; it is all about Jesus. And Jesus never fails. Here is what He said:

> The thief [meaning Satan] comes only to steal and kill and destroy. I came that they may have life and have it abundantly. I am the good shepherd. The good shepherd lays down his life for the sheep. (John 10:10–11)

Forgiveness, assurance, and the inner working of the Holy Spirit that produces faith and gives us LOVE, JOY, MEANING, and HOPE—this is our prescription for health.

Chapter Two
Confession is Good for You

Christians do not have to pretend they do the right thing all the time. Perfect we are not. Neither do we have a "license to sin," as some accuse us. Our desire is to be careful followers of Jesus. Before going any further, it is important to consider a very interesting paradox we find in Scripture.

The Paradox Involving Confession

A paradox is two truths that run parallel to each other like the rails of a railroad track. They are laid right next to each other but never intersect. This is a fair definition of a paradox. And confession definitely involves a paradox.

One rail of the tract is the fact that all of our sin was placed on Jesus when He died on the cross. Our sin was then buried, or put away, with Jesus in His tomb. It is utterly and completely gone—all of our sin, past, present, and future. Yes, it is all covered by the blood of Jesus.

The second rail is that we are to continue to confess our sin, despite the fact that all of that sin has been forgiven. Paradox?

This is where personal and ongoing confession comes in. Let us examine a key passage of Scripture, that of 1 John 1:8–2:2.

First, 1 John 1:8–10:

> *If* we say we have no sin, we deceive ourselves, and the truth is not in us. *If* we confess our sins, he is faithful and just to forgive us our sins and to cleanse us from all unrighteousness. *If* we say we have not sinned, we make him a liar, and his word is not in us.

The "ifs" in italics (my work) above are in the Greek grammar called "future more probable" conditional clauses. So then, it is possible that a Christian may say they have no sin, but if they do, it is a big mistake. Such denial means having to carry guilt around, and doing so eventually damages us both spiritually and emotionally. Over time, guilt multiplies, self-condemnation sets in, and relationships are undermined.

We see the paradox then: We are forgiven yet still need to confess our sin—both at the same time.

Later on, John writes, "In this is love, not that we have loved God but that he loved us and sent his Son to be the propitiation for our sins" (1 John 4:10). Out of God's love for us, He does not want us to carry around the weight of unforgiven sin. This is why confession is good for us. Our ongoing sin is not to be ignored, it is to be confessed. And not just simply, "Lord, forgive me, a sinner," but to name them one by one, the circumstances and instances, including details.

Confession, One to Another

James, the half-brother of Jesus and first pastor of the Jerusalem Church, wrote, "Confess your sins to one another and pray for one another, that you may be healed" (James 5:16). This opens up something different from the foregoing. Now confession is made directly to others, even and especially to those against whom we have sinned. Instead of settling for broken relationships, the attempt is made to heal breaches as they develop, and we all know that they develop.

Caution is advised when it comes to confessing sins one to another. The gifts of wisdom and humility are vital here. We are careful not to accuse, blame, or gossip in making confession. In addition, over-sensitivity must be avoided, but healthy relationships, especially within the family and the church, are critical.

The Great Judge is Merciful

Christians do not have to hide from God nor anyone else. Even if one commits a really egregious sin, there is still forgiveness. This is a lesson I learned from talking with convicts at San Quentin Prison over thirty-four years as a volunteer there. Murder, rape, and other such crimes are no barrier to total and complete forgiveness, though it may take a long while for the freedom of forgiveness to settle within. Our Father God never stops loving us, and we cannot fully grasp this; we can only struggle to believe and accept it as enormous truth. While others remember our sin, even accuse and blame us far into the future, the Judge of all does not. He actually forgets our sin.

One of the enduring images I have carried with me over the decades is that I am standing before God at the Day of Judgment, but He does not see me, since Jesus is standing right in front of me. The Judge only sees Jesus His beloved Son. I am completely hidden in Christ.

Knowing this solid biblical truth, I have confidence to live my life freely without the burden of guilt and shame. I have done some pretty ugly things, actions others will still bring up, for whatever reasons, but I know I am covered in the shed blood of Jesus. And this is not a psychological invention of mine; it is a truth straight from the Word of God.

Second, 1 John 2:1:

"My little children, I am writing these things to you so that you may not sin. But *if* anyone does sin, we have an advocate with the Father, Jesus Christ the righteous."

Notice the "*if*" again. It is that same construction, a

third-class conditional clause as before. John means that we likely will sin, and if and when we do, we have the best lawyer there is to argue our case, which always results in complete acquittal. Jesus is our advocate, our counselor, our attorney.

As we mature in our Christian lives this truth becomes very precious to us. We go through difficult times, sometimes lasting over considerable periods of time. For whatever reasons, we do some very stupid things, so much so that we are tempted to think our heavenly Father is angry at us and rejects us. NO, and NO, and NO. Wrong thinking. This is the way of a fallen world, but we are not *of* the world any longer. We will not let anything or anyone separate us from the love of Christ. Here is how Paul put it in Romans 8:38–39:

> For I am sure that neither death nor life, nor angels nor rulers, nor things present nor things to come, nor powers, nor height nor depth, nor anything else in all creation, will be able to separate us from the love of God in Christ Jesus our Lord.

What does this all mean? One thing is clear: we do not fear to confess our sin to God. He is the ultimate Father.

I have five children, and I would never want to add to their burden, if they did something egregious. My desire would be to make whole again, and this is the desire of our Father who is in heaven.

A Final Word of Encouragement

Confession is good for us. No matter how often, and it is certainly daily, we have full access to the throne of grace. Jesus took upon Himself all our sin, so it is gone forever already, and the delight of the Father is to remind us of that very fact.

Chapter Three
Accepting Forgiveness

However it developed, we humans are driven by our feelings. What forgiveness feels like is an issue that must be examined.

"I don't feel forgiven" is something that runs through most of our minds. The consequences of stupid things we have done remain with us. I have in my memory bank images of things I have done that I am deeply ashamed of, and try as I might, I cannot erase them. These have become part of who I am. And maybe, just maybe, that is a good thing.

Forgiveness—Feeling or Fact?

If I *feel* I am forgiven, does that mean I am forgiven? If I don't *feel* I am forgiven, does that mean I am not forgiven?

What part do our emotions play in our Christian life? It seems for many that emotions and feelings are akin to spiritual realities that seem to affirm or not the working of the Holy Spirit in our lives. Relying on our emotions and feelings, however, might open the door to error and the possibility of being deceived. After all, where in the whole of the Bible do we find that our feelings dictate spiritual realities?

If forgiveness is a feeling, then we cannot ever be sure we are forgiven, since our feelings are notoriously fickle. What a terrible place to find ourselves! Guilt can be unrelenting and tortuous; it can drive us mad. Since we know this cannot possibly be the will of our Father in heaven, we must rethink our view of forgiveness.

Forgiveness, biblically speaking, is a fact and not a feeling. It is firmly based upon the work of Jesus Christ dying on the cross. He put away our sin, completely. The author of Hebrews wrote, "He [Jesus] has appeared once for all at the end of the ages to put away sin by the sacrifice of himself" (Hebrews 9:26).

Jesus, dying and receiving all of our sin upon Himself, was buried, and all our sin was buried with Him. Certainly, we will admit this great reality is beyond our ability to grasp. Yet the putting away of sin is central to all of Scripture from Genesis to Revelation.

The Imagery of Baptism

The definition of "baptized" is plunged, dunked, or immersed. Biblical baptism, in which the believer is plunged into or dunked or immersed in water, is the image of what happens to the Christian at the moment of conversion. Water baptism is not a magical ritual whereby sin is removed and cancelled; rather, it is a dramatic representation of a spiritual reality. Here is the person standing in a river, a lake, a stream, an ocean, a swimming pool, or a baptistry in a church building, and this person is laid under the water—buried in the water and raised up again.

The point is that sin is buried; it is gone, washed away; it is all and completely forgiven. Upon this truth we take our stand.

The Accuser

Christians have an enemy who accuses them of not being Christians and safe in Christ. This threat is rendered impotent based on Revelation 12:10 and numbers of other passages:

> Now the salvation and the power and the kingdom of our God and the authority of his Christ have come, for the accuser of our brothers has been thrown down, who accuses them day and night before our God.

To which accuser are we most vulnerable, ourselves or Satan? The answer is both/and. No matter which, the accusations come at us. In my case, when I hear anyone slam me for things that happened in the past, sometimes decades ago, I do not think they are demonized. However, I do question whether they know the power of the cross and the extreme love the Father has for His children.

Acutely Aware of Sin

Early on in my Christian walk, I was devastated when the accusations came. Now I may cringe a bit, but I am more sensitive to my sin and see it more clearly now than ever before. Early on, I even questioned my conversion. Now I rest in the fact that I have been born again and my sin is washed away and forgiven. This is where I will stand.

Once again, we encounter an unresolvable paradox. Totally forgiven yet needing to confess our sin—two truths existing side by side but never joined or resolved.

Here are some ways I experience my own sin, little things that happen so innocuously: a slight, a boast, an exaggerated statement, leaving out matter that should have been stated, not spending enough time with someone, being in a hurry to do what I want to do, a judgmental look or thought, and the list could go on and on. I am busy sinning.

What will I do? Without kneeling, closing the eyes, or folding the hands, I say a little prayer in process, "Please forgive me Father, have mercy upon me."

In the parable of the Pharisee and the Tax Collector ("The Publican" in the KJV) in Luke 19:9–14 is an ancient prayer: "God be merciful to me a sinner" (v. 13). Our congregation at Miller Avenue prays an ancient version of it every Sunday. We have put it to music and sing it twice, just before we receive the Bread and the Cup. Our version is, "Lord Jesus Christ, Son of God, have mercy on me, a sinner." This is, as far as I know, the oldest Christian prayer found outside the Bible itself.

Jesus' conclusion to the parable, and the primary point of the comparison is, "I tell you, this man went down to his house justified, rather than the other" (v. 14).

"Justified" is a perfect passive participle. The grammar Jesus used is very important. Perfect tense means that an act has occurred whose results go on forever. Passive voice means that the subject is acted upon, meaning the subject did absolutely nothing to earn any result.

Tax collectors were Jews who sold out to Rome and extorted money beyond the normal tax due—big sinners in everyone's eyes. This traitor went home completely forgiven, though others might accuse him and the devil attempt to defeat him. Regardless of the tax collector's feelings, his sin was gone. And it was all an act of God.

Accepting Forgiveness

By faith we accept the forgiveness we have in Christ. If forgiveness is something we can achieve on our own, then forgiveness is fleeting. I have to challenge myself to stand at the foot of the cross when I am tempted to accuse myself or accept accusations from our enemy and those who are under his sway. Despite my feelings and regardless of the unbiblical bits of data that flit through my brain, I know I am forgiven.

Standing firm on this reality keeps us healthy. It is biblical Christianity all the way.

Chapter Four

Growing into the Fullness of Christ

We start out as new born babes, then little by little we grow up. This is true physically and also spiritually. Like many children, I thought I knew most everything after I first completed reading the Bible all the way through. At age twenty-one I was some years away from being even physically mature, much less anywhere close to being spiritually mature.

When I was thirty-one, after a whole decade in the Faith, I thought I was a spiritual giant. I did already have a MDiv degree from a top-flight seminary, had been ordained, and had pastored a church. I even was the head of a growing ministry and would occasionally see my picture in a newspaper. I was a big deal, or so I thought. But, what goes up must come down. And I hit hard on the rocks when that happened to me.

Things hadn't changed much by age forty-one, or fifty-one, though there was some modicum of growth. Sixty-one, seventy-one, looks like I'll notch eighty-one, God willing, and I will still be working on growing up into the fullness of Christ.

How about you? Can you make an honest assessment

of yourself? If so, you are blessed indeed. Let's look at some verses that may speak to us.

1 Peter 2:2:

> Like newborn infants, long for the pure spiritual milk, that by it you may grow up to salvation.

I Corinthians 3:1–2:

> But I, brothers, could not address you as spiritual people; but as people of the flesh, as infants in Christ. I fed you with milk, not solid food, for you were not ready for it. And even now you are not yet ready.

Hebrews 5:12–14:

> For though by this time you ought to be teachers, you need someone to teach you again the basic principles of the oracles of God. You need milk, not solid food, for everyone who lives on milk is unskilled in the word of righteousness, since he is a child. But solid food is for the mature, for those who have their powers of discernment trained by constant practice to distinguish good from evil.

It is not wrong to admit we are not yet mature, in fact, it is an indication of a developing and healthy maturity. A Bible college or seminary degree does not automatically make us mature. I had written a systematic theology by age thirty-five and had five books published by major publishers, but I was a long way from mature. I had yet to go through a divorce, which necessitated my resignation from a thriving ministry I had founded coming out of the Jesus People Movement.

There is a real need for us to be honest with ourselves. Otherwise, we cannot live a healthy Christian life. Too often churches and Christian organizations lose patience with those of us who act immature and cause difficulty, and to a degree this is understandable, but we, brothers and sisters, cannot be afraid to make an honest estimation of who we are. To do otherwise is to harm ourselves mentally and emotionally.

A Very Good Reason

One of the reasons for this book is the hope that the church of Jesus Christ in our own day would be mature to the point of helping those who are in the midst of the often-painful struggles that characterize spiritual growth. At minimum, Christian leaders need to be aware that there is a maturing process. Pastors must understand this, or they will be ill-equipped to help the infants develop beyond that stage.

It is essential to understand that we grow up at different rates from one another. I have been guilty of expecting others to be further along in their growth process than they were and thereby ended up judging them. I will admit right now that as a pastor I have damaged others by expecting too much from them. And looking back, I wish others would have been more patient with me as well.

In the years of my struggles and rebellion, I was, as it is said, "thrown under the bus." During the times I needed brothers and sisters in Christ the most, I was ostracized. And as painful as it is to admit, I had done the same in earlier times.

Since we grow up at different rates, we must be patient with ourselves and others and not expect conformity. This does not mean that we should excuse sinful behavior. We cannot rush growth, yet at the same time, we should strive for it.

The Work of Christian Leaders

Leaders in the body of Christ have a responsibility to help those under their care. Paul puts it so very well in Ephesians 4:11–13:

> And he gave the apostles, the prophets, the evangelists, the pastors and teachers, to equip the saints for the work of ministry, for building up the body of Christ, until we all attain to the unity of the faith and of the knowledge of the Son of God, to mature manhood, to the measure of the stature of the fullness of Christ.

It is within the fellowship of a body of believers where the best opportunity for growing up in Christ exists. The old principle of "iron sharpening iron" applies; this dealing with others is where growth takes place. The lone wolf Christian will grow very slowly, if at all. We need others around us—people who know us, people who are willing to invest their lives into us—in order grow up, even if by friction.

Yes, it is risk taking, but it is natural. The older I got the more I collided with my parents and my brothers. It was all good for me, though I did not understand the dynamics of family life. At school there were even more clashes, and these proved to be invaluable. Others in the pews, people from different backgrounds, differing points of view on politics, theology, and more—iron sharpening iron.

Physical and Spiritual Maturity

Growth depends on a number of factors: food, exercise, love from the family, encountering life, and learning to cope. Refusing to give up when we are defeated, struggling through difficult times like "dark nights of the soul," learning how to love, learning to deal with our own rebellion and sin, experiencing disappointments, coping with illnesses, both physical and emotional—all are essential to developing a healthy maturity.

A Slow Growing Up

Our growing up comes a little at a time and is almost imperceptible. And our growing up is His gifting to us, as John expressed it in John 1:16: "And from his fullness we have all received, grace upon grace."

Not until we are in His presence, in our resurrection body, experiencing full joy and maturity, will we be all that we can be.

Chapter Five

Having Meaning and Purpose

Most of us live with our basic needs met. Food, clothing, and housing are common and accessible to the majority in the developed world. If an individual or family needs assistance with these, government agencies and other institutions are there to help with some kind of safety net.

Having work to do, a reasonably safe environment in which to live, and the prospect of reliable health care, we have a higher standard of living than most of those who have walked the earth. Then there is the possibility of enjoying life and the capacity to be creative and expansive, even the potential for fame and fortune. Is that enough?

There Is Something More

One may live a middle or even upper-class life but still be empty. There is something more, and that is to live with meaning and purpose.

My family of origin lived the standard middle-class life. My assumption was that I would get married, have kids, work for a living, retire, and hope to live into my eighties. This is what my father and his two younger brothers hoped to do as well. And with the exception of my youngest brother, we were headed well into that pattern.

After high school and my stint in the military, I saw that I could live the normal, American, middle-class life. Having nearly completed an MA degree in psychology at Sacramento State, I planned to be a school psychologist.

Yet, deep inside of me I wanted—rather, I needed—more.

Mid way through my four years as a medic in the Air Force I became a Christian at age 21. I was already married with two children, and it had looked like plans were going along just fine. However, my view of the world and of myself began to change. Where I was headed was not enough.

The Call

Given my fear of public speaking I never considered being a preacher. I was scared to death of taking speech class and had to take it at a community college, because speech class was a requirement to receive an AA degree. No speech class meant no four-year school. Finally, I faced it and finished it at Napa Community College in Napa, California, and was allowed to head off to UC Davis and later Sacramento State.

Just as I was about to graduate with an MA in psychology something happened to me—I felt strongly called to go to seminary and study for the ministry. I could not shake it, and my wife was not terribly happy about it. Each passing day the desire to study the Bible grew, until I gave in and talked to my pastor about it. The day after my enlistment in the Air Force ended, I moved my family onto the campus of Golden Gate Baptist Theological Seminary in Mill Valley, California.

It has not been a smooth ride, with much turmoil, many disappointments, and a number of personal failures, but that call is still deep inside me.

The Universal Call

Few are called into what we call the ministry. Most of us are not called to this work, but all Christians are called to grow up into Christ, follow Him, and obey His commands. This means that for all Christians, there is meaning and purpose.

First, we are called to love God with all that we are. We generally do not even know what that means, though occasionally in my life I have thought I knew. It is a slow study, and the words escape to clarify here.

Growing up into the fullness of Christ might have been simpler had I not read the Gospels—Matthew, Mark, Luke, and John—but I did and I do, so I continually discover that Jesus is very incredible and mostly beyond my mental grasp. I must admit that I merely stumble along. But He is nevertheless there leading and urging us onward—this Savior, Master, Lord, the great Shepherd—and we are the little lost sheep. We have only to follow Him who is always out ahead of us calling us to Himself.

Work to Do

Jesus has graciously given us work to do. Imagine laboring in the Carpenter's workshop, learning to use His tools, receiving instruction on how to build His way! Not a day goes by but that it seems there is something completely new to discover. This is a life-long challenge and adventure.

All of us are called to love Him with all that we are and to love our neighbor as ourselves. We looked at this in the first chapter. This commandment alone requires life-long effort. Then there is the command Jesus gave us to serve Him. That is what we are—servants, even slaves, whose primary work is to do what He has called us to do.

When I was in seminary, Professor Francis DuBose spent an entire semester expounding on and emphasizing one single verse. That verse, John 20:21, had already become a favorite of mine and became more so as I dove as deep as I could into its heart. The verse came at a time when I was just beginning my street ministry in the Haight-Ashbury District of San Francisco, and it became an anchor for me:

> *Jesus said to them again, "Peace be with you. As the Father has sent me, even so I am sending you."*

Consider—"as the father has sent me"—and that we are called to do the same. I knew the words from years past, but I did not really know the implications. By the working of the Holy Spirit it dawned on me that I am already sent. The King of glory sent me. It still thrills me.

The Great Commission

According to the Gospel of Matthew, Jesus' last words to His disciples are,

> "Go therefore and make disciples of all nations, baptizing them in the name of the Father and of the Son and of the Holy Spirit, teaching them to observe all that I have commanded you. And behold, I am with you always, to the end of the age." (Matthew 28:19–20)

"Go" is the first word in the sentence, and it is, in the Greek, indeed a command to do something: go, go, go. It is a command to the whole of the Church and to each one individually. We are to go and go everywhere. Christians have fairly well done this, and we are doing so more today than at any other time in the history of the world, given modern technology.[1]

The goal of going and doing is to make disciples. This is an inclusive term; one cannot be a disciple until he or she is born again, converted to Christ. Once the saving message of the Gospel is proclaimed, boldly proclaimed, then the discipleship process begins and never ends. Yes, I am still being discipled; I continue to learn, as do all genuine Christians.

We are not called to be entertained and appeased, and we are not called merely to meet the needs of others but to speak to the one issue above all others, the gift of salvation by grace alone.

We are called to be disciples. We are to study Jesus, learn from Him, and follow in His footsteps. One of the initial steps in discipleship is baptism. This is a landmark for many of us; it was for me. In my baptism I had the glorious opportunity to do something Jesus said to do. This is where it starts for so many. At our baptism we openly acknowledge that our God is Triune—Father, Son, and Holy Spirit.

Notice now that as we obey Jesus' command to go and make disciples, He is with us all the way.

---

[1] For instance, our small congregation presently produces three television programs that are available all over the world via the Internet. These can be found by going to YouTube and typing in my name, Kent Philpott.

Here then is meaning and purpose of the highest order. To perpetually wonder what life is all about is not good for our mental and spiritual health. Being a follower of Jesus is life at its best. There is nothing better.

We Christians, we have it all.

Chapter Six
Keeping in Fellowship

Christians are part of a very large family. There are brothers and sisters in Christ all over the globe. There are elders, middle aged, young adult, teens, adolescents, and children. Some are new believers, others are old soldiers. Some are flourishing, others are struggling with various issues. Some live well, some are starving. There are those who are honored and those who are dying, because they refuse to renounce their faith in Jesus.

At the church I pastor there are precious folks who suffer from mental illness. There are those who show up who are not yet converted. Some are even trouble makers with a rebellious spirit.

Every church is a mixed bag. We will only be wonderfully perfect when we dwell eternally in the presence of God. Until then, anything can happen, and I did not understand this in my early days in an actual church.

I was shocked to find I was sitting in the same pew with some real odd balls, weird people, yet there they were, and it would have been risky to ask them to go elsewhere. I remember one guy who really troubled me; his very presence irked me. Later I found out he was suffering from a diagnosable disorder and was doing the best he could. In the local church we cannot assume everyone is completely sin-free and angelic.

The World-Wide Family

Every time my wife and I attend a major conference of Christians with people from all over the world present, like the National Religious Broadcasters gathering or the International Christian Retail Show, we meet brothers and sisters in Christ who are actively engaged in some form of ministry.

What has always interested me is that the subject of what denomination or church one belongs to does not come up most of the time. Sometimes I can tell by the garb worn that I am speaking with a Roman Catholic or an Oriental or Eastern Orthodox Christian. Other than that, we simply recognize that we belong to Christ.

That there are differences, even some very large ones, is well known. Despite doctrinal disagreements, we all share a basic historical and biblical theology. While I love to talk about our varying views, it can be done knowing we are ultimately in fellowship with one another, thus no one needs to feel threatened or defensive. Christianity is not a cookie-cutter thing, to borrow an old cliché, but this is a fact, and being in the Body of Christ is a very wonderful thing.

Fellowship is Biblical

> And they devoted themselves to the apostles' teaching and fellowship, to the breaking of bread and the prayers. (Acts 2:42)

This is Luke's description of what it was like in the early days of the Church. What strength there is in uniting together in the name of Jesus! It is plain from Paul's letters to various churches that there were certain troubles that needed to be addressed. Yet, most of these churches survived for centuries, and the Gospel message went out from them vigorously.

From the passage quoted above we see that fellowship is mentioned second. The Greek for fellowship is *koinonia*. We get the word coin as in a nickel or dime from the basic word. It means having things in common. And what we have in common is Jesus and His salvation. We are literally "in Christ"—Jesus is the head and we are the Body.

The Express Purpose of God

Read what the Apostle John wrote to the churches under his care during the last decade of the first century:

> That which we have seen and heard we proclaim also to you, so that you too may have fellowship with us, and indeed our fellowship is

with the Father and with his Son Jesus Christ. And we are writing these things so that our joy may be complete. (1 John 1:3–4)

Notice a very important fact in the passage: proclamation of the Gospel is directly linked to fellowship. John clearly points out one of the consequences of the proclamation of the message of Jesus is fellowship.

Not only that, but the fellowship is with the Father and the Son, the result of which is joy.

This joy is inexpressible, that is, we do not have words to describe it. The Apostle Peter wrote, "Though you have not seen him, you believe in him and rejoice with joy that is inexpressible and filled with glory" (1 Peter 1:8). The joy experienced alone is wonderful, and in the fellowship of brothers and sisters in Christ it is truly inexpressible. And this is the will of God for us.

Since 1963 I have enjoyed the fellowship of other Christian people. Not always, but most of the time, I look forward to driving to church to be with the congregation on Sunday morning. During the week I will miss them, and when someone is not present, I miss them more. It is not that way with other groups with which I am commonly involved. There is just that certain un-namable something about being with those who love Jesus.

Remain in Fellowship

Not all Christians gather together on Sunday morning. Some meet at other times. There are fellowships that meet several or more times a week, some just once, but most are in fellowship weekly. This is the historical and biblical norm, but in our pressure packed world this is not always possible. If I could so arrange, I would lobby for a weekly Sunday morning gathering as the norm, because meeting together in fellowship is a necessary and healthy part of the Christian life.

Let me return to a theme I spoke of earlier: Christians are not always easy to get along with. This is actually a good thing and for at least two reasons.

One, we learn how to love others, as Jesus told us to do. It is easy to love and be in close fellowship with compatible, comfortable friends we have known for a long time. But in a fellowship of believers, there are those who are hard to love and those we just don't know well. And this is good for us, because it moves us out of our comfort zone and stretches us to grow in love.

Two, we learn how to pray for others' needs, which takes the focus off ourselves. Narcissism is a big word today, and of course, we are not, the other guy is. Or so we imagine. We are to pray for each other, listen to each other, come along side those who are hurting, and like the good Samaritan, help bind up their wounds. Yes, a concentration on others beyond ourselves is healthy.

The Perfect Congregation?

Is there one? Certainly in heaven, but not on this planet. How could it be otherwise?

When I was a non-Christian, I assumed Christians were perfect. Where I got that from I do not know. I had a friend named Jim when I was fifteen, and he went to church and even invited me to come along. Then I saw him do something I thought was awful, so I dismissed him and his Christianity right then and there. "Well, if that is what Christians do, I sure am not going to be one of those hypocrites."

Hypocrites! Yes, we all are. We espouse the highest ideals and usually fall very short of them. Part of being a Christian is learning to be honest with ourselves. We know we are sinners and continue to sin, though we increasingly want to turn away from it, but we are fallen creatures living in a fallen world. Understanding this is incredibly healthy.

We can admit the truth about ourselves because we are greatly loved by God and have been declared both now and forever forgiven and saved to the utmost.

We need not constantly look for the perfect church. Oddly, a church is both perfect and imperfect at the same time. Realizing that this is so means we do not roam from church to church until we find one just right.

My counsel is to find a church that identifies with historic, biblical Christianity, one where the Bible is taught and preached. A solid congregation is one that focuses on bold proclamation of Jesus and the making of disciples.

Chapter Seven

Expect Opposition

Those who call Jesus Lord have always been subject to persecution, bias, and bigotry from those who are yet in their sin and estranged from the love and fellowship of God. They must do so out of fear of judgment and shame for their sin. Even when we do not utter a word of judgment, non-believers may have a sense of conviction of sin in our presence. Merely because we do not join in with what is displeasing to God is enough to trigger their negative emotions.

We will have opposition, mild and severe, even within our own households. Jesus said this would happen.

Prior to my conversion to Christ in 1963, I confess I did oppose, persecute, and make fun of Christians. I did not know why I did so, except that there was this certain something that agitated me about them. None of them did anything deliberate to incite my unpleasant reactions; in fact, we were more than mere acquaintances. But any time they attempted to tell me about Jesus, I rejected them and the topic of conversation.

My Old Friends

It was during my service in the Air Force that I became a Christian myself, and on my next leave I drove home to Sunland, California. I walked in the back door of the old house on Whitegate Avenue and found six of my old buddies waiting for me. My mother had arranged this little party.

Right away, one of them handed me a beer, and as he did so he whispered in my ear that they had paid for a hot Hollywood prostitute for me.

Settling into the family room where we had spent so much time when we were high schoolers, one of them said, "Well, Kent we hear you got religion."

I can still see myself sitting in the middle of the big couch, a friend on either side of me. Slowly I started to formulate an answer. As I write this now, I am experiencing some of the shock that came over me back then.

My first word was, "Yes." Then I took about five minutes and gave to them my first attempt to be a witness for Christ. They listened in silence. I could hear my mother puttering around in the kitchen; I knew she was hearing what I was saying.

Without a word, three of the six friends stood up and left the house. It was the last time I ever saw them. The three who stayed, Bill, Dick, and Larry, became my lifelong friends, but only Dick became a follower of Jesus.

My mother never did become a Christian, though she was a faithful member of the local Methodist church. As far as I know, she rarely attended services, but she nevertheless sent in some money every month.

Unprepared

It took me a long time to get over the rejection. No one ever told me such a thing could happen, especially from old friends. But there it was.

Before long I realized that simply believing in Jesus as Savior and Lord could get me into trouble. I was unprepared for the rejection, and that is why I am including this chapter. It is healthy to know and be prepared for what may come when others find out we are actual born-again Christians.

Let's take a look at Scripture on this subject.

Jesus Was and Is Opposed and Hated

Jesus was opposed throughout His ministry. He was finally betrayed, arrested, beaten, scourged, and executed. If this happened to Jesus, can we expect to be treated much differently?

In some countries of the world being a Christian means being despised, persecuted, disenfranchised, and much worse. In the USA, where there is rule of law and a majority of the population still identifies as Christian, that has not precluded a growing bias against those of us who are biblically-oriented Christians. To stand for biblical principles and ethics will eventually, unless there is a great and powerful moving of the Holy Spirit, bring more antagonism from non-Christians. We must realize this possibility. And what do we do in reaction to this?

Persecution Will Come

The three words above serve as a description in the *English Standard Version* of the Bible for Matthew 10:16–25. Jesus said He was sending us out as sheep in the midst of wolves. Thanks a lot, we might say. At least it is full-disclosure; we know from the beginning what we are getting into, and this helps us prepare for and adjust to opposition that will come our way.

Jesus even said, "you will be hated by all for my name's sake" (Matthew 10:22). Toward the conclusion of the passage, in verse 25b, He said, "If they have called the master of the house Beelzebul, how much more will they malign those of his household."

In speaking of the events that will occur toward the end of human history, the runup to the second advent of Jesus, He said, "Then they will deliver you up to tribulation and put you to death, and you will be hated by all nations for my name's sake" (Matthew 24:9).

In Luke's version of the Sermon on the Mount, we find these words:

> Blessed are you when people hate you and

when they exclude you and revile you and spurn your name as evil, on account of the Son of Man! Rejoice in that day, and leap for joy, for behold, your reward is great in heaven; for so their fathers did to the prophets. (Luke 6:22–23)

The Apostle John, who knew what he was talking about because he experienced it, wrote, "Do not be surprised, brothers, that the world hates you" (1 John 3:13).

Not to know these unhappy realities would be devasting to us. For all these years now, to one degree or another, I have experienced anti-Christian bias and prejudice. Often, those who treat us as such do not even understand what they are doing. They are blind to their own hard hearts.

Christians Build Strength

Christians who are aware of opposition, however, are better able to meet the challenge. It is like going to the gym for weight training—it builds up our strength. In addition, when we are prepared for what might happen, we are not shocked or knocked off our game when trouble comes our way on account of our testimony for Jesus.

Neither do we become paranoid, always expecting the worst. Since most everyone knows I am a Christian pastor, I do experience prejudice, but in this I rejoice.

At the same time, because others know where I stand, it is not unusual for people to seek me out to hear more about the Gospel or receive counsel. It is really a very interesting two-edged sword.

At this point in my Christian journey I have settled into the whole lifestyle; it is not boring being a Christian.

The Christian Reaction

Peter wrote: "Do not repay evil for evil or reviling for reviling, but on the contrary, bless, for to this you were called, that you may obtain a blessing" (1 Peter 3:9). Whether we are looking for a blessing or ever obtain a blessing that we recognize as such, we do not repay evil for evil. Thus, we maintain a healthy conscience. We are not fearful, we are fully ready, and we actually expect opposition.

The Apostle Paul was a persecutor of Christians to the point of imprisoning them and having them killed. Paul knew persecution from both sides. His word on these points can be a great encouragement to us. Here now is Romans 12:9–21:

> Let love be genuine. Abhor what is evil; hold fast to what is good. Love one another with brotherly affection. Outdo one another in showing honor. Do not be slothful in zeal, be fervent in spirit, serve the Lord. Rejoice in hope, be patient in tribulation, be constant in

prayer. Contribute to the needs of the saints and seek to show hospitality.

Bless those who persecute you; bless and do not curse them. Rejoice with those who rejoice, weep with those who weep. Live in harmony with one another. Do not be haughty, but associate with the lowly. Never be wise in your own sight. Repay no one evil for evil, but give thought to do what is honorable in the sight of all. If possible, so far as it depends on you, live peaceably with all. Beloved, never avenge yourselves, but leave it to the wrath of God, for it is written "Vengeance is mine, I will repay, says the Lord." To the contrary, "if your enemy is hungry, feed him; if he is thirsty, give him something to drink; for by so doing you will heap burning coals on his head." Do not be overcome by evil, but overcome evil with good.

Chapter Eight

End Times

In Matthew 24, Mark 13, and Luke 21 Jesus revealed all that the early Church would face, as well as what the Church throughout history could expect.

Wars and rumors of wars, nation against nation, kingdom against kingdom, earthquakes, famines, Christians being led astray, false teachers performing incredible miracles—all these, Jesus declared, are only the beginning of woes.

Jesus went on to say that "You will be hated by all nations for my name's sake" (Matthew 24:9), and He also stated, "And then many will fall away and betray one another and hate one another. And many false prophets will arise and lead many astray" (Matthew 24:10–11).

We know this is coming, so we will not be shocked or surprised when we experience it personally.

The question is, do we see this end-time scenario being played out right now? It is possible, but nevertheless, we are standing on solid rock and will not be moved.

Those who trust in Jesus will not be panic stricken or overcome with anxiety as others will. Instead, we will look upon world events as news of interest but not as something that could overwhelm us. We know that God is in control, and even if the worst should descend upon us in this earthly life, we belong to Him and will spend eternity in His presence.

Stressful Living

Few would argue that we are not now living in stressful times. My personal evaluation is that these are especially difficult times, and I am aware that I am more anxious now than in previous years. The digital, techy age is fun and exciting, mostly, but it has made the world a smaller place, we are aware of hideous events taking place daily everywhere, and it adds to our inability to cope with it.

I read two newspapers every day, the *San Francisco Chronicle* and the *Marin Independent Journal*. I watch NBC, CNN, FOX News, PBS, and a few other news programs regularly. I am informed because I have to be. When I am with others, Christians and non-Christians, as a pastor I need to be aware of local, national, and world events. It is expected of me.

Some, even fellow believers, are startled that I am not shaking in my boots when we discuss world and national events. It gives me opportunity to explain the peace I have in Christ. This witness will be even more potent as time goes on.

In California where I live, marijuana is legal, and hundreds of thousands use it every day, including some of my friends. In our county, half the high schoolers are vaping. They tell me it helps relieve the stress and pressure they are under. And these are not old hippies but regular folk who live and work and go to school in the "age of anxiety."

Our world can be dangerous. Innocent people are killed every day someplace in the good old USA while minding their own business, even when securely in their own homes.

Does this signal the end of the age?

"No one knows the day and hour."

The statement above is Jesus' own (Matthew 24:36). There was a time early in my Christian life when I had charts on the wall of my office; I actually thought I could figure out when Jesus would return. A number of modern 'prophets' have announced dates, to the embarrassment of us all. Let's heed Jesus who said that no one knows the day and hour. We don't know, and we don't need to know. We simply go about the business of preaching Christ to the lost and discipling those who are found.

What we do know is what we disciples are to do. We have our agenda. It matters not what goes on in the world around us. No, we pay attention and are aware, but what goes on in the world is of secondary importance to our mission.

A Christian Witness

I am reminded of the words of Martin Luther's great hymn, *A Mighty Fortress Is Our God.* If ever a Christian was attacked by enormous forces it was Luther, the one who laid the foundation for what we refer to as The Reformation. Here now is the complete text of that hymn:

> A mighty fortress is our God,
> A bulwark never failing;
> Our helper He amid the flood
> Of mortal ills prevailing.
> For still our ancient foe
> Doth seek to work us woe—
> His craft and pow'r are great,
> and armed with cruel hate,
> On earth is not his equal.
>
> Did we in our own strength confide,
> Our striving would be losing,
> Were not the right man on our side,
> The man of God's own choosing.
> Dost ask who that may be?
> Christ Jesus, it is He—
> Lord Sabaoth His name,
> From age to age the same,
> And He must win the battle.

And tho' this world, with devils filled,
Should threaten to undo us,
We will not fear, for God hath willed
His truth to triumph thro' us.
The prince of darkness grim,
We tremble not for him—
His rage we can endure,
For lo, his doom is sure:
One little word shall fell him.

That word above all earthly pow'rs,
No thanks to them abideth;
The Spirit and the gifts are ours
Thro' Him who with us sideth.
Let goods and kindred go,
This mortal life also—
The body they may kill;
God's truth abideth still:
His kingdom is forever.

"Nothing can separate me from the love of God in Christ Jesus our Lord."

Above are the words of the Apostle Paul. Martin Luther, in my thinking, might have borrowed something from Paul when he wrote his wonderful and powerful hymn. I am thinking of Romans 8:31–39. In this section, Paul asks a series of questions and provides answers for each:

What then shall we say to these things?

If God is for us, who can be against us?

He who did not spare his own Son but gave him up for us all, how will he not also with him graciously give us all things?

Who shall bring any charge against God's elect? It is God who justifies.

Who is to condemn? Christ Jesus is the one who died—more than that, who was raised—who is at the right hand of God, who indeed is interceding for us.

Who shall separate us from the love of Christ? Shall tribulation, or distress, or persecution, or famine, or nakedness, or danger, or sword? As it is written, "For your sake we are being killed all the day long; we are regarded as sheep to be slaughtered."

No, in all these things we are more than conquerors through him who loved us.

For I am sure that neither death nor life, nor angels nor rulers, nor things present nor things to come, nor powers, nor height nor depth, nor anything else in all creation, will be able to separate us from the love of God in Christ Jesus our Lord.

What Is Healthy about these Great Truths?

Christians will be fearful and stressed and anxious, because we are people like everyone else. However, we have something solid on which to stand and reflect. We have the Word of God and the testimony of one from the earliest generation of Christians, that being Paul, and also the words of Martin Luther who lived some 1,450 years after Paul.

We also have the testimony of hundreds of others who were persecuted and were martyred down through the centuries.

Not that Christians won't suffer from anxiety in this world of chaos, but we have an assurance that cannot ultimately be taken from us. I confess I am prone to anxiety and have been since I was fifteen years old; it has never completely left me, but I rely upon the testimony of Christians who have suffered more than I have, which includes Jesus Himself, Paul, and countless others.

I will be shaken from time to time, but my foundation in Jesus remains firm.

Chapter Nine

Suffering Is to Be Expected

By "suffering" I mean physical, mental, and spiritual.

In the last chapter we looked at what we cannot ignore or dodge—the persecution and turbulent times that Jesus assured us would come, both in the present and in the future. As the saying goes, "The devil be busy." We have lived in the age of anxiety since the Fall, as recorded in Genesis chapters one through five.

Suffering—all three types above—are common to humankind. No one is immune, yet as a pastor, I have constantly witnessed that Christians are shaken when something bad happens to family members, friends, and themselves. This is a common reaction, even from Christians who are biblically literate. It is an emotional reaction, usually of short duration but sometimes longer.

The Bible is quite reality oriented, and nowhere does it state or even vaguely imply that Christians get a pass from suffering. Since a reality orientation is wiser and saner than the opposite, this shows that biblical Christianity is healthy. Jesus, Paul, Peter, and so on, suffered very much, and no excuses were given. Every form of suffering is part of the human condition.

Physical Suffering

When an accident, criminal act, war injury, or disease results in a physical disability, lives change and sometimes dramatically. Family members are impacted as well. We might wonder, "Is this the will of God?" "Why did this happen to me?" "Am I being punished?" "I thought God was a good God."

Sometimes nature takes its course, and a natural healing takes place. Medical technology is often able to bring healing, and God still heals in miraculous ways, as I have witnessed on dozens of occasions. But even in the days of the Jesus People Movement, when miraculous healings occurred more often, not everyone was healed. Without exception, even those who were healed sooner or later experienced some form of physical problem including death.

Sometimes the sufferings last and last. There is no promise in Scripture that "good" people won't suffer. If there were, the Bible would be a dangerous book. Since the author is God Himself, who made us in His image and determined the boundaries and scope of our living, it is built into the process that physical suffering is to be expected.

Most people understand this; it is when we have false expectations that difficulties arise.

I know that I am going to be ill. Right now, I have a thyroid problem and am glucose intolerant, so I take serious medications, because if I am not careful, I will develop diabetes. Plus, I need to wear glasses and do not hear so well anymore. Should I grumble and complain? If I did, it would not be an expression of a healthy mind, and it is to the mind we turn next.

Mental Suffering

Yes, Christians experience mental distress, even mental illness. I have several good friends, some of them in the professional ministry, who struggle with bipolar illness, both bipolar 1 and 2. In addition, I am close to people who suffer from depression, obsessive/compulsive disorder, schizophrenia, and other diagnosable disorders. In fact, we have two support groups in our congregation, one for relatives of those who suffer from mental illness and one for peers, those who actually have a mental illness.

During the 1970s, while pastor of the Church of the Open Door in San Rafael, I operated a Christian counseling center. Four days per week, six appointments per day, for ten years I met with people who needed the "talk therapy" style of counseling. I loved the work. My college background in psychology helped immensely, and I learned a great deal about mental illness.

It was not unusual for pastors of churches, sometimes from neighboring counties, to come for counseling.

Some of them struggled from high states of anxiety, and a few suffered from serious bipolar conditions. (At that time the term was manic-depression.)

A huge obstacle was being able to admit to suffering from a mental disorder. Over time these dear people came to realize they were not being punished, had not sinned, and were in fact not responsible for the illness any more than one is blameworthy for having cancer or the flu. Once this fact was admitted, treatment could begin.

In that era there was a substantial stigma associated with mental illness. To counter this, I spoke of the fact that I was prone to anxiety. From time to time I mentioned that as a teenager I was a hypochondriac, that my youngest brother was diagnosed with schizophrenia when he returned from the Vietnam War and later killed himself when he went off his meds. I spoke of these things many times, and for a reason. I wanted those who suffered from mental illness to understand they could talk about their disorder and seek treatment openly.

Before we come to Christ, we are convicted to repent of our sins; therefore, we have to admit to them. So too, to get help for any illness we must admit to having it and then seek aid. This is healthy. We are Christians by identity, yet as human saints we carry with us the effects of the Fall.

Spiritual Suffering

"The dark night of the soul" is an expression that refers to spiritual struggles or battles, during which one suffers defeats to the point of considering suicide. I have had this happen to me. If you have not gone through such a dark night, it may yet come.

There is a hint or two in the Apostle Paul's writing that he went through some excruciating trials. He was very forthright in admitting his pain, and this is healthy. Did Jesus not do the same? We read of His anguish in John 17. Take the time to read it and you will see. (Remember the sweating.)

In my experience I have counseled any number of people who thought God had abandoned them. The heavens seemed veiled in lead. God was nowhere to be found; no comforter was comforting.

Spiritual suffering often accompanies physical and/or mental suffering. It does not require much understanding to see how the illnesses can overlap and influence one another.

It is healthy to be mindful that we are God's beloved children, loved by the Father, Son, and Holy Spirit. And I mean "mindful" in the biblical sense. I am mindful when I reflect on the fact that Jesus paid the price on the cross for my sinning. I think of the reality that I am indwelt by the Holy Spirit. I meditate on the truth that I have a home in heaven and that nothing in all creation can take it from me. My name is written in the Lamb's Book of Life. Yes, that settles it, and I am mindful of this. It is so very healthy to set aside a time in each day, if only five minutes, to apply these great truths to our lives.

Suffering does not erase the fact that we Christians are hopeful people.

Chapter Ten

The Great Hope

For most people hope means a "wish," hoping for something they want to happen but not having the confidence that it will. This idea does not come close to the biblical concept of hope.

A Sure Thing

We look forward to being in the very presence of God. This will take place, either at the moment of our death, or at the second coming of Jesus at the end of the age.[1]

From the very earliest strata of biblical material, the first several chapters of Genesis, we find that the whole purpose for creating humans in the image of God was to have fellowship with the Creator God.

---

[1] To be published at a future date is *The Paradoxes of God*. In regard to our being present with God in heaven, Scripture has two different ways of saying it. One, at the moment of our death, we are right then in the presence of God in heaven, fully complete with a resurrection body. Then the Scripture also teaches that the resurrection, with body, occurs at the time of the return of Jesus. Both are true at once. We know that God is not bound by time but lives outside time, but we live within time. It is the difference between *kairos* and *chronos*; *kairos* being God's time, *chronos* being our linear time.

We will never comprehend this; it is way beyond our understanding. But there it is. "So God created man in his own image, in the image of God he created him; male and female he created them" (Genesis 1:27). Then He had fellowship with Adam and Eve, walking and talking with them in the "cool of the day." Preposterous, absurd, unimaginable, but real and true.

Of course, there was a big problem. We disobeyed the single commandment given to us. My use of the plural, "we" and "us" is not poor grammar on my part. We were *in* Adam and Eve, we inevitably share in their "fall," and we share in their exclusion from Paradise. We have been living "east of Eden" ever since.

However, due to His great love toward us, He sent His Son Jesus to take away the cause of our separation from Him.

Fellowship Regained

Please take the time to carefully read through the passage below. It is from the first letter of the Apostle John, chapter one and verses one through four. You will find the core of all that is the will of God for the creatures made in His image.

> That which was from the beginning, which we have heard, which we have seen with our eyes, which we looked upon and have touched with our hands, concerning the word of life—the

life was made manifest, and we have seen it, and testify to it and proclaim to you the eternal life, which was with the Father and was made manifest to us—that which we have seen and heard we proclaim also to you, so that you too may have fellowship with us; and indeed our fellowship is with the Father and with his Son Jesus Christ. And we are writing these things so that our[2] joy may be complete.

Our hope is not a wish. It is a future reality. Our fellowship in the congregation of God is a foretaste of that which is to come.

Certainly, the fellowship we now enjoy, which can be very wonderful, has its flaws and limitations. After all, we are still in the flesh, however sanctified we might suppose we are.

Now But Not Yet

Our fellowship with God is not perfect. Every one of us is acutely aware of this. Even if we were to live in a cave like a monk in the desert and contemplate all things Godly from sun up to sun down, we would still have a sense that something is missing, something is not quite right.

---

[2] Though "our" is the preferred reading, many reliable New Testament manuscripts have "your" instead of "our." The "our" would include "your." The point is that all Christians, in whatever era, are included.

We must come to terms with this in order to be healthy. There is a gap apparent; there is a longing for closer, deeper fellowship. And herein is a danger.

On the planet we cannot breach the gap; it exists. The shamans, the occult practitioners, Hindu and Buddhist holy ones, and even actual Christians will attempt to bridge the gap through trance states and contacts with the supernatural. Contact is indeed made with the supernatural, but not with the God of Scripture; rather it made with demonic spirits. This is not healthy; it is the very opposite.

Our hope is partially deferred right now. We are to wait patiently for the full revealing of the Son of God. We await our being caught up to be with Him in the air, clothed in our resurrection body. We have already been invited to the marriage supper of the Lamb, the table is set, and we will be seated at a time we know not.

Nothing Can Separate Us

Biblical hope is assurance, not wishing. It is concrete and certain.

In Romans chapter eight verse 39 Paul states unequivocally that absolutely nothing can separate us from the love of God in Christ Jesus our Lord. *Not even we ourselves!*

Right, not even we can separate ourselves from God. Why? Because we did not save ourselves; we have been saved. All the religions of the world teach that we are able to save ourselves (sadly even some within the broad Christian family think so), or at least, that we cooperate in that saving. God works, I work, and the outcome may be salvation. This, gladly, happily, is not biblical Christianity. Paul makes this clear in this famous chapter eight of Romans:

> For those whom he foreknew he also predestined to be conformed to the image of his Son, in order that he might be the firstborn among many brothers. And those whom he predestined he also called, and those whom he called he also justified, and those whom he justified he also glorified. (Romans 8:29–30)

A Closer Look at the Reason for Our Hope

God *foreknew* us. Prior to the creation of the universe, God knew His sons and daughters. Of course, we will not grasp this until we are in heaven, and maybe not even then. This is how enormous God is. We cannot measure Him by our standards and understandings.

Knowing moves to *predestination*, a logical step. God predetermined our salvation—thankfully, since we cannot possibly save ourselves. No one has lived a sinless life—not close, not even for a day.

Foreknew, predestined, then *called*. The process of coming to Christ as Savior demonstrates this calling. We are convicted of our sin. Prior to that we are either not aware of our separation from God, due to our sin, or we fight against it and simply try hard to be better people. Then it becomes inescapable: we are lost and alone and without God.

Justified comes next. This is our seeing that Jesus is the Savior. After failing miserably at every attempt to save ourselves, and there are many roads people follow in this effort, we have a revelation, slight or huge, that Jesus has taken our sin upon Himself. "Just as if we had never sinned" is sometimes offered as a definition of "justified." What happens to us is more than that—but it is close.

Now we are indwelt by the Holy Spirit of God. We have been moved from death to life, and not on the basis of anything we have done, but solely upon what God has done. Our sin has been nailed to the cross and we bear it no more, to quote a great old hymn. A done deal.

Glorified follows. This is understood as the growing up into Christ through the working of the indwelling Holy Spirit. God calls ministers to equip believers for the work of ministry and for building up the Church, "until we all attain to the unity of the faith and of the knowledge of the Son of God, to mature manhood, to the measure of the stature of the fullness of Christ" (Ephesians 4:13).

Sanctification—growing up in Christ—is always an incomplete process this side of the coming of the kingdom of God, but it is ongoing with every follower of Jesus.

This is the normal and healthy Christian life, a hope that does not fade nor disappoint.

Chapter Eleven

Peace Beyond Understanding

Christians may enjoy wonderful, peaceful, and reflective meditation. The contemporary term "mindfulness"[1] works for Christians, since it refers to bringing our thoughts and feelings into our devotional practices. We have long practiced the study of the Bible and prayer during devotional periods. Throughout our long history, meditating on the work and wonder of the Triune God is widely known.

For years I kept to a devotional life, from Monday to Friday, reading through the Bible, followed by meditating on something I saw in the passages I read, followed by a time of prayer. Using a prayer list where I recorded the date of a prayer, the nature of the prayer, then a space for an answer and that date, a good hour would pass, but it seemed like a few minutes.

Nowadays, like many pastors, my devotional life is

---

[1] Mindfulness means engaging one's mind into something real. It is definitely not a blanking out of the mind. It does not depend on a trance or passive state of mind. It is taking stock of one's presence, how one is sitting, breathing, feeling, and so on. It is active, conscious, and very important to our physical, mental, and spiritual life.

focused on what I am preaching, teaching, or working on for a television program. And I never have enough time for it all; other things enter in.

A Peaceful Start to the Day

Whether short or long, spending time with the Word of God has great value. My best time is early, even before the newspaper and coffee. Or after. No matter.

I like to think through my day, take out my calendar, plan what I can, and reflect on what I am likely to expect during that day. Most of the time I look ahead at the rest of the week as well.

Some of what I have to do may provoke anxiety in me, but I do my best to alleviate it by knowing I have to do certain things, go certain places, and talk with certain people—some of which I would rather not have to do. I just face it. Once in a while I suspect that an issue or two may be particularly risky for me, and when I see one, I talk to my wife about my feelings.[2] This is all good.

I tend to treat the late evening in a similar way. A glance at the calendar, checking out any late messages on my computer, shutting that down, grabbing the latest

---

[2] If you are alone, there might be someone to call—sometimes friends set this up between them; sometimes people interact with an on-line counselor.

book I am reading, and staying with it until the words get blurry.

Rest, Food, Exercise, Work

There is more to being spiritual than being mindful and meditative. Yes, we must get our rest and eat right, if possible. Exercise, consistent and strenuous, is absolutely essential. And if we are so blessed to have work to do, we work with enthusiasm.

In 1978 I began going regularly to a community gym, trying to be there Monday, Wednesday, and Friday. If I missed some days, no big deal, but I kept at it, and over the years it has been good for me. Not everyone can get to a gym, so if possible, walking around the block or up and down the street is very helpful. We have to move to be healthy.

Romans 5:1

> Therefore, since we have been justified by faith, we have peace with God through our Lord Jesus Christ.

You may rest, eat right, exercise regularly, and work as you can—these alone will not give you peace, a peace that resides in your inner core.

The peace Paul speaks of in Romans 5:1 is peace with God. Peace is the opposite of enmity, which can be against a relative, a friend, life itself, even ourselves.

Prior to finding peace with God through forgiveness of our sin we have no real peace, even if our lives seem to be going along nicely. Once we grasp that we are loved of God, who has wiped away all our sin, past, present, and future, we have a new lease on life. We can be at peace in the midst of conflict.

Notice in the passage above, Paul speaks of being "justified by faith." Someone will say, however, "That means I have to have faith, but I have no faith." This is not all Paul has to say about faith, happily. Here is the rest of the story:

> For by grace you have been saved through faith. And this is not your own doing: it is the gift of God. (Ephesians 2:8)

I have to emphasize the phrase, "and this is not your own doing." If I had had to save myself by having enough faith, and even a little scrap of faith, then all would have been lost for someone like me. Mostly I have little faith; I knew this then and I know this now. What I lack, God gives me. He gives me faith.

I admit I don't get it; it makes little sense to me. But there it is. It is a *gift* of God.

When people tell me they have no faith, I will sometimes say, "Ask for it. Ask God to reveal Jesus to you. Ask Him to open your eyes and let you see the cross of

Jesus." That may seem a little strange to some, I know, yet I have seen this sort of prayer answered numerous times.

Why is it that God gives saving faith? Paul answers this question in Ephesians 2:9, the very next verse. Speaking of grace, or God's giving faith, he says, "not a result of works, so that no one may boast."

Religion Is about . . .

Isn't religion all about being good people, helping others, being loving and kind, working to do the right things, following the commands of God, and on and on and on?

The answer is NO!

Well, you could say that is the essence of *religion*, but it has nothing to do with biblical Christian faith. Working to earn favor with God will eventually drive us crazy.

Our Peace . . .

The peace we have with our God is beyond understanding. I do not want you to think I understand it all, but I trust what the written Word of God tells me. Jesus has saved me and forgiven all my sin, and now I am indwelt by the Holy Spirit as I await being in the presence of God forever and ever. Amen.

Chapter Twelve

The Best Sex

God created us humans, male and female, says Genesis 1:27. This means, among other things, that sex is built right into the essential nature of who we are. No sex, no more people.

The author of Genesis continues in the next verse: "And God blessed them. And God said to them, 'Be fruitful and multiply.'"

Sex is blessed; God's seal of approval on sex between the male and the female is loudly expressed in the very first chapter in the Bible. Sex and its results are called being "fruitful."

Rounding out Genesis chapter two we find God making this most incredible statement:

> Therefore a man shall leave his father and his mother and hold fast to his wife, and they shall become one flesh. And the man and his wife were both naked and were not ashamed.

"One flesh"—is this a discreet description of sexual coupling? Likely, and we notice that they were naked without shame. I suspect they were enjoying lots of wonderful sex.

But this changed, and quickly.

Something Terrible Happened

Three chapters into Genesis we find that something terrible occurred. We call it the "Fall," and as you've noticed, the race is still falling. One little command was broken; in fact, it was the only command in existence at the time. It was simply not to eat of the fruit of a particular tree.

That tree, the Creator God said, was "the tree of the knowledge of good and evil" (Genesis 2:17). He warned them that if they ate of it they would surely die.

They ate of it, thanks to the inspiration of a lying serpent, but rather than keeling over dead, they suddenly had knowledge of good and evil. It overwhelmed them, and when "they heard the LORD walking in the garden in the cool of the day" (v. 3:8), they hid themselves among the trees of the garden. The LORD pursued them and called out to the man, who replied, "I heard the sound of you in the garden, and I was afraid, because I was naked, and I hid myself" (v. 3:10).

We have been hiding ever since.

What Happened Next?

The human experience of sexuality changed radically. Instead of being a normal and healthy part of life, it has so often been smothered with an unholy embrace. Without need to cite statistics and report on countless numbers of case studies, we agree that our sexuality is confused and diseased.

On a nude beach everyone knows they are naked. Many folks, especially ex-hippies, have told me over the decades that it is fun but not good for you. While exhilarating and hormone charging, there is something that goes on with the brain's chemistry that harms us, similar to what viewing pornography does.

Porn viewing and engaging in sexual behavior other than that which is intended by the Creator God produces guilt, shame, anger, hyper-sexuality, even addiction to sex, all of which dehumanizes a person. One may be driven to greater and greater excess or risky behavior that damages relationships and undermines one's sense of self, even if it is all or mostly unconscious.

Is this too harsh a judgment on my part? Is it that I have just not dropped enough acid, smoked enough dope, or refused to adopt a more liberated mindset?

It might be that soon the only voices who speak out against unbiblical sexual practices will be those who adhere to a biblical worldview. The culture will sweep the rest into conformity with the prevailing trends and celebrate, even legalize, forms of sexuality the Scripture condemns.

It is likely that a time is coming when even thinking, much less communicating, that homosexuality and bisexuality are against God's law or harmful to people's well-being, will be categorized as hate speech, even hate crime. *1984* and *Brave New World*, here we come. Even so-called free speech rights will be eroded and denied in favor of the sexual free-for-all agenda.

One wonders, why would this be so? Why the dramatic departure from normal, biblical sexuality? The answer may be the inward fear and guilt people sense who then need to find a rational excuse for their behavior. Another answer may be that most people no longer have a clue what the Bible says about this subject, only what they see and hear in the media and from their own crowd. We are rapidly becoming a culture that has lost its moral compass.

Will We Ever Know the Pleasure of True and Godly Sex?

Probably not is my view; others may disagree, but I do not see a movement toward a time like we had in the garden before the Fall. The so-called Age of Aquarius certainly wasn't it. Not that this generation of people on the planet is any worse than any other, and there have been some really gross eras in our history, but I have witnessed a general decline, especially in first world nations.

No one is as pure as the wind-driven snow—not me, not you. We have simply been exposed to so much garbage that the lovely days of innocence will not reappear; however, we can move in that direction.

This brings up the question of whether those who follow the commands of God as found in Scripture might enjoy sex as once intended.

Sex Can Be Healthy

My experience is that Christians usually enjoy good sex, maybe the best sex. And sex is really good for us. Biblically oriented sex is the best sex, since it has a better chance of being free from guilt and shame.

Did you notice that Adam and Eve were naked and did not even know it? We will never see those days again. But we can come close, or closer than some might think.

Okay, let's look at what it can be like.

One, admit the Creator God's ideal is that sex is between a man and a woman who are married (remember Genesis 1:27–28 and Genesis 3:23–25).

Two, grasp that married means having sex with only one another. They are not having affairs or "open" marriages, not watching X-rated stuff on a screen, not experimenting with other forms of sexuality—they are devoted to each other. These people will have a lower chance of divorce, since there is a strong sexual and love bond between them.

There is nothing to hide, nothing to be found out, no guilt, no shame, and they can go at it as much and as often as they want to. Real freedom, real pleasure.

How Can this Be?

I can hear it now. "It's too late for me; I am dirty, and there's no going back." Wrong!

Go back and read the chapter on forgiveness. You, too, can experience the joy of being forgiven by the Creator God. You have eaten of the forbidden fruit and have been forced out of the garden, but Jesus Christ opens the way back in.

Jesus is the way, the truth, and the life (John 14:6). Turn away from the sickness around you and turn toward the Savior. It is never too late. Jesus is always knocking on the door.

Chapter Thirteen
Being Alone

Is it true that over one half the households in America are headed by singles? Regardless of the actual numbers, it is fact that many people live alone. This seems to be trending upward. Why is this? The reasons are many:

- Our population is aging, and older people's spouses die.

- Many are waiting years longer than before, unlike my generation, to get married.

- The cost of raising a family is high and growing more so every day, especially in the large metropolitan areas like the San Francisco Bay Area.

- Many who would marry simply will not settle for less than true love.

- Women no longer assume they need to depend on a man for income, so they stay independent and in careers.

- Men no longer need a woman to provide homemaking, cooking, etc. when it is easy to purchase those services and products.

- Couples divorce at an approximate rate of 50%.

- Many people would like to be with someone, but for many complicated reasons, it never happens.

Since 1986, at Miller Avenue Baptist Church where I am pastor, we have conducted a divorce recovery workshop. We hold four eight-week workshops every year. Thousands have been a part of it. We have found that, typically, women wait longer to remarry than men do. It is not unusual that many attendees of the workshop decide they would rather be alone than go through the agony of another unhealthy relationship.

Aloneness Versus Loneliness

In week five of our divorce recovery workshop we talk about the difference between aloneness and loneliness. The newly separated can easily experience loneliness, which is a painful emotional state and can last for years. It can lead to depression, substance abuse, and other forms of destructive behavior. Our goal that fifth week is to help people move from a state of loneliness to aloneness.

Aloneness is the goal, but it can be elusive. One of the reasons for this is that the ending of a relationship often cuts one off from others, especially if the couple had friends and family who don't stay connected to both spouses.

However, I have noticed it helps quite a bit, if a person is a Christian and has other believers with whom to be engaged.

Whether a person finds him or herself alone and lonely due to the ending of a relationship or for some other reason, deliberate steps must be taken to move from loneliness to aloneness.

Being Alone as a Choice

Once in a while, for spiritual reasons, men and women desire a life dedicated to contemplation, service to the poor, and other forms of sacrificial ministry. That studio apartment, single bedroom duplex, or one room cottage becomes a sacred space much like a convent or monastery. Indeed, we have a new breed of people amongst us who treasure being alone for spiritual reasons.

Some say God gives them a special grace gift to live alone and be celibate. I think of St. Francis of Assisi for one, and there are many others whose names were never published who sought and highly valued the contemplative life.

Within the Roman Catholic Church and the Oriental and Eastern Orthodox churches have been many who have either lived alone or within a cloister of others who cherished being single. Yes, but also among Protestants, even Baptists like myself, many are finding a rich and rewarding life being alone. I have at least four friends in a particular ministry who have each been single and celibate for decades. They each have rich social lives and cherish their common mission work.

Never Really Alone

The Christian is never alone, in at least two ways.

First, consider Matthew 28:19–20:

> Go therefore and make disciples of all nations, baptizing them in the name of the Father and of the Son and of the Holy Spirit, teaching them to observe all that I have commanded you. And behold, I am with you always, to the end of the age.

"With you always." Since we are indwelt by the Holy Spirit upon our conversion, Jesus can truthfully say this. The Holy Spirit, the Spirit of Christ, the Spirit of Jesus (all synonyms)—with us and in us until the end of the age or our last moment on the planet.[1]

We actually cultivate a relationship with the Creator God. It is not unlike the experience Adam and Eve had before the Fall. God walked and talked with them in the cool of the day. One has to be careful here, as some contemplatives have gone a bit overboard. The main forms, in my estimation, for building a relationship with our Lord are through prayer, study of the Word,

---

[1] In chapters 14, 15, and 16 of John's Gospel we have the most beautiful account of the presence of the Holy Spirit, the Comforter, the Paraclete, the Counselor presented by the beloved Apostle John. I suggest spending some precious hours reading and reflecting on these passages.

and reflecting upon the great truths of that Word.

Mysticism we do not want, but rather down to earth, normal Christianity—none of the St. Theresa of Avila or St. John of the Cross approaches. Even Richard Foster wandered too far in this direction. (Though I'm sorry if I offended some here, I must sound this warning.) These dear ones moved from normal contemplative to spiritism and unbiblical mysticism.

Second, we are called to community. Upon conversion we are placed by the Holy Spirit into the Body of Christ. We belong to Jesus in two ways. We are His personally, but we are also placed into fellowship with other believers, becoming parts of His Body. The Church is not an afterthought on God's agenda.

A congregation is a bunch of sinners in one place. This can be dangerous! And we have an enemy, Satan, so where would he go to destroy his enemy? Yes, he would head for the nearest congregation and preferably one that is evangelical in nature. There's no sense in warring against those who are not a threat to him. Therefore, one of my definitions of a flesh and blood actual congregation is that it is a "mine field." This is coming from a pastor of churches with over fifty years of experience. I say "mine field," because I have been blown up a few times and have contributed to others being blown up as well.

I have seen plenty of messiness. One time, in 1980,

I packed up my Bible and vowed never to attend a church again. That lasted for less than a month. I found that I wanted to hear the message of Jesus preached and taught in real time, not just on the television or over the radio.

"Iron Sharpening Iron" was a ministry I was involved with for thirteen years at San Quentin Prison in Marin County, California. The other name we had for it was "Man to Man Ministry." The idea was that we, in our interaction with each other and with the convicts, "sharpen" our Christian lives. We wanted to hone the dull edges and apply fire to harden the iron. It was rough work going cell to cell talking with guys whose lives were a complete disaster. We were tested more than the cons, because much of the Christianized approach I had been exposed to would not work there; I had to be real. This only happens in association with other Christians who are serious about following Jesus.

Another reason a real-life congregation is dangerous is that brothers and sisters in Christ range wildly in their spiritual development. There are those who are not yet born again. I was a member of the First Baptist Church of Fairfield, California for nine months before I was actually born again, and I caused my share of trouble. Then there are "new babes" in Christ who are still in their stinky diapers. Then the toddlers, the teens, the young bucks, and all the rest.

All the while, iron was sharpening iron, and this would

have been impossible had I never darkened the door.

Alone and Connected

Being alone does not mean completely alone. And it is in being alone that some of the strongest, most wonderful friendships are developed.

Again, I draw on my experience as a pastor. In our small congregation there are several precious people who have deep and lasting friendships with others, which are just as family-like as could be. Some of the best friendships I have ever seen are with those who live alone.

If you are alone, and if you do not want to isolate, find a church with which to connect. Do not think you will find the perfect church, since there is no such thing. As the saying goes, once *you* are a part of one, there goes its perfection!

Being part of a church, an assembly of believers, a congregation of saints, is part of the normal Christian life. It is a step toward health to be a part of one.

If at first you don't succeed, keep looking and praying.

Chapter Fourteen

Anxiety and Worry

"Do not be anxious about anything," Paul wrote to the Philippian Church. Instead of being worried, we should bring our concerns to God by means of prayer and supplication with thanksgiving (see Philippians 4:6).

And we do, and it helps. We have a relationship with God; we are indwelt by the Holy Spirit and are thus connected. Scripture urges us to pray, so we do, and we see many answers to our prayers.

Sometimes I do not see the answers as they occur. It may take months, even years, before I see that a prayer was answered, and this is without talking myself into it. It simply becomes apparent. At the same time, I still worry. And it is likely that you do, too.

To Be Like Jesus

Based on my extensive reading of the Gospels and preaching verse by verse through Matthew, Mark, Luke, and John at least twice each, I have not seen that Jesus was ever worried like I get worried. Even reading 'in between the lines,' Jesus was calm, cool, and collected, at least until the night before His crucifixion. Even then He gave His concerns to the Father and accepted His will.

Jesus was well aware of the dangers He faced. Three times He announced to the Twelve that He would be killed. He knew what was coming. The kingdom was squarely upon His shoulders.

He did not fear His opponents, and He did not withdraw from them except to pray. Once or twice, to protect His disciples, He got out of harm's way by going north to Galilee. He was vulnerable, with only two swords in the group's armory, but He faced every challenge.

To Be Honest about It

I am not like Jesus much of the time. When I was younger, I was less anxious. Now, in my seventh decade, I find I have lost a certain amount of strength and flexibility. Yes, I still go out to the prison to do baseball, coach high school baseball, stand in front of the television camera, and preach away on Sunday morning, but I can tell I have changed.

What to do about it is a serious question.

Helpful Hints?

First, I am not going to conceal my weaknesses. I do talk about them, in prayer, with my wife, and with a close friend or two. I can be honest with God, since what would I want to conceal from Him, and how could I do so if I tried? I recall these words from a hymn: "He knows my every weakness." Neither the title of the hymn nor the author comes to mind, but I attest to what he or she meant.

Second, all my sin is forgiven. The devil cannot get at me. I just keep confessing my sin (see 1 John 1:8–2:2), walk away forgiven and blessed, and keep going.

I have a habit I am trying to break. I speak of myself in negative ways: "I am a bad man." "I never get it right." "I ought to be fired." "I need to resign from the church." "I am just your average jerk." (This last one I have said from the pulpit a number of times, I must confess.)

This is not a healthy habit, and writing this chapter helps remind me that saying such things to myself is not healthy, either mentally or spiritually. By God's grace I am stopping this practice.

Third, my Christian friends are an encouragement. The brotherhood of believers can be so supportive. I have learned not to hang with those who like to criticize and be judgmental; this is not the way of Christ at all. I even wonder if those who delight in pointing out our flaws are really born-again Christians. It is more likely that those who desire to encourage and build up are the real brothers and sisters in Christ.

Four, I might be a little 'off' sometimes, and so I know I need to be humble and not hesitate to ask for forgiveness. However, this can be overdone to the point of ridiculousness. We do not want to be so overly sensitive that we shut down, fearful to do or say the wrong thing. The issue here is our own personal acceptance of who we are. We are not actors on a stage or job seekers trying to impress. We are who we are, and our job, one of them anyway, is to like ourselves.

Five, be able to laugh it off. We do odd things and say things we wish we had not. So what? We need not take ourselves so seriously. We have to be free to be ourselves.

Six, we can be self-affirming, "Yes, as a matter of fact, I manage a baseball game very well." "I think my books serve a real purpose and many people like them." "My preaching is improving." "This is the best period in my life."

We try not to be worried about making mistakes along the way or worried about what others think of us. We want to be the best of who we are, but we don't always succeed. Okay.

Casting Our Cares

What the Apostle Peter wrote for us in his first letter to the churches, chapter five verses six and seven, is so very helpful:

> Humble yourselves, therefore, under the mighty hand of God so that at the proper time he may exalt you, casting all your anxieties on him, because he cares for you.

Let us focus here only on the "casting all your anxieties" part of the sentence. Here is our word, anxiety, in the plural—anxieties. Does Peter expect the believers he is addressing to have anxiety? The answer is easy.

Just because one is a Christian does not mean one does not get anxious. Let us avoid the mistake of thinking, "Well, if you worry you cannot be a Christian."

Where does this thinking come from? Not from the Bible. Not from the mainstream teaching of the Church down through the centuries. Not from the Holy Spirit. It emanates from somewhere else, but discussing its source is not worth the time and trouble.

A Last Word

Here it is, and this is not the first time to make this point, but it needs to be made again. Cast all our cares, concerns, worries, anxieties, fears, and whatever else is skulking around—cast them on Him. And by "Him" we mean the Triune God, Father, Son, and Holy Spirit.

Will you be able to do this? Probably not to the extent you would like, but you hope to obey the Word, and this is what counts.

If necessary, make a list of your worries. Each time you pray, get the list out and bring each one, again and again, in prayer to the God who loves you.

I doubt I will ever get to the place where I have put all my anxieties and worries behind me. What is foremost is that I keep doing what Scripture invites me to do anyway.

Chapter Fifteen
Sabbath Rest

> Remember the Sabbath day to keep it holy. (Exodus 20:8)

"Sabbath" means rest. The Sabbath day is a day to be kept holy, and primarily this means not doing any work on that day. Rest is the whole thing, and it reflects God having rested on the seventh day after He created the universe.

Resting the body, the mind, and the heart is healthy. Getting good sleep is as important as exercise and eating right. A healthy mental and emotional dimension is just as crucial. A sound body and mind go together.

There is something of equal if not greater importance—the spiritual dimension. We may be resting the body, sleeping and eating well, getting enough exercise, with well-adjusted thoughts and feelings, yet we can be unhealthy if we do not have spiritual health as well. And spiritual health is what the Bible brings to us.

There Are Two Sabbaths

First, there is the actual ceasing from work or labor. This is the intent of the fourth of the Ten Commandments given to Moses by God on Mt. Sinai around 3,500 to 3,800 years ago. Over time many dozens of subsidiary laws were developed that were designed to keep anyone from even coming close to breaking the primary laws. By the time of Jesus, the "hedge around the law" consisted of hundreds of extra ordinances that needed to be observed so that the primary law might be kept. These had become quite burdensome over time.

The first job I ever had was delivering kosher foods to Jewish households on Friday afternoons. This gave me a firsthand opportunity to learn about all that went into the preparation for the evening Shabbat meal. Preparing the meal was labor intensive, and it took an experienced woman to complete it successfully. Try as hard as they might, few could boast they kept perfect kosher homes.

The Jewish Sabbath begins sunset Friday evening and extends to sunset Saturday evening.[1] When the sun slips below the horizon, the Sabbath is on and no work is to be done, not even turning on a light switch after dark Friday evening. This is all to obey the commandment from God as delivered to Moses, and thus to all of Israel.

Is there more to it than this?

Second, there is a fuller meaning for the fourth commandment.

---

[1] The actual onset of the Sabbath and its ending are variously stated. The movement of the moon also comes into play. My description is generalized.

Last Sunday someone asked me, "Pastor, why don't you rest on Sunday instead of working like you do preaching and everything." My reply was, "I am resting; yes, it wears me out, but I am resting. I am resting in Jesus and doing what He called me to do."

My work is such that I rarely have a complete day off, especially with cell phones and computers in constant proximity. It is frankly impossible for me to take an entire day off. Yet, I manage to clear away an evening here, an afternoon there. But I am "resting" 24/7.

The Sabbath laws are impossible to keep, especially in an era such as ours. We recall that one of the purposes of the Law of God is to show us we are law breakers and thus in need of a Savior. If we depend on our keeping all the laws to be acceptable to the Creator God, we are indeed in way over our heads.

Since God is holy, sin (unholy acts and thoughts and intentions) cannot be in His presence. To be with Him in heaven, our sin must be put away. And this is exactly what happened when Jesus died on the cross. Here now are a few passages from the Hebrew Bible that make this clear:

> But he was wounded for our transgressions; he was crushed for our iniquities; upon him was the chastisement that brought us peace, and with his stripes we are healed. (Isaiah 53:4–5)

> Yet it was the will of the LORD to crush him, he has put him to grief; when his soul makes an offering for sin, he shall see his offspring; he shall prolong his days; the will of the LORD shall prosper in his hand. (Isaiah 53:10)
>
> And he shall bear their iniquities. (Isaiah 53:11)
>
> Yet he bore the sin of many and makes intercession for the transgressors. (Isaiah 53:12)

Isaiah was looking ahead to what the Messiah would accomplish. The Christ, a title derived from the Greek language and synonymous with Messiah, took our sin upon Himself and died in our place, thus making it possible for us to be forgiven.

Just how, then, does this work, we might ask. This question is the whole thing.

Jesus Is Our Sabbath Rest

We rest in the Person and Work of Jesus the Messiah. Jesus, our Passover Lamb, shed His blood to cleanse us of all our sin. He died in our place and took away the penalty of sin, which is death—the final and ultimate outcome of our sinning.

Yes, this runs counter to the general view of all of the religions developed in human history. At best, they focus on self-improvement, doing good to others, being kind, helping the poor, and caring for the environment—all of which are good and right and are activities and deeds all of us should attempt to do. However, and this is a big however, these have nothing to do with forgiving our law breaking.

The Greatest Health

However fit and physically healthy we may be, how emotionally and mentally stable and secure we may be, unless we are spiritually healthy, we are in the poorest of health.

Sin is what separates us from God. It does so both now and forever. With Jesus as Savior and Lord, we have peace with God right now. And when we leave the planet, we have peace with God forever and ever. To neglect this is most dreadful.

There is a tragic sense of life, and we all know what that is after we have lived a few decades. But there is a greater loss, which is being forever driven from the presence of God.

A Summary

Living by the tenets of biblical Christianity is healthy living.

By means of regularly confessing our sin we are free from guilt and shame. What a burden it is to carry around the weight of unforgiven sin. Oh, I remember my sin, and others may remind me from time to time how awful I was, or I am, but the One who counts has utterly and completely forgiven me.

I am accepted by my Creator God and can accept myself and the fact that I am a son or daughter of God.

I continue to grow up. Where I am right now I will not be tomorrow; the Holy Spirit is working on me.

Now I have a reason to live; having purpose and meaning is huge, and every day I have an opportunity to share the Gospel message with others.

I am not alone; I am part of the world's largest family. Some don't care for me much, but I have tons of real brothers and sisters in Christ.

Opposition is something I expect, living in the fallen world. How could it be otherwise? But I know it is present and it does not intimidate me in the least; in fact, it spurs me on.

The end of the world does not threaten me. Jesus said His followers would face great difficulty at that point, but that it would not last long, and He would be with us through it all. So, bring it on.

Life happens to us all, and I will suffer. No one gets by unscathed, and as I get older, family and friends become disabled and die. We simply get old. But again, we are not alone.

I have real hope, not a wish, that the best is coming. That best is the current reign and return of Jesus and the assurance of salvation. This is not hoping and wondering what the real outcome will be; Jesus is Savior and Lord now and forever.

I am no longer at war with God. It is done, the peace agreement has been signed, sealed, and delivered.

Yes, I am tempted to worry and be anxious; who is not? When I get rattled and distracted, fearing what is going on with me and my world, I can look to Jesus and He will make me strong.

Biblical Christianity is healthy. How incredible, we have the best of it all both here and now and forever. We have every reason to give thanks to our God.

Postscript

In physics we hear of the "Unified Field Theory" or the "Theory of Everything" or the "Grand Unified Theory"—and the search for this theory has gone on ever since Albert Einstein first mentioned the possibility about a century ago.

Those who are followers of Jesus know of a unified field theory, too. The equation may look like, "To God be the glory." For us to seek to glorify God in all that we do and all that we are is our life theory of everything and is our ultimate health.

This does not mean that by living to honor, praise, and glorify God He is obligated to bring us health in all its dimensions. No, it is not a formula, recitation, or set of laws but a gift of grace. It is not by works.

Many who have discovered the grand theory of everything have lived difficult lives, which from outward appearances was anything but healthy. Yet, when viewed from the perspective of eternity, it is real health.

As Christians, People of the Book, we define healthy in a different way from others, and this is what I have attempted to do with this Little Book. Every chapter expresses aspects of what it is to live for the glory of God.

What is the alternative? Well, to live for ourselves is the

obvious short answer. Some commit to a political ideology, even a strong man. And such living leads them only into a brick wall. The creature serving the creature is what you have then. How empty, boring, and unhealthy.

In Christ we have a higher calling—to live for the glory of God. This is our theory of everything.

www.ingramcontent.com/pod-product-compliance
Lightning Source LLC
Chambersburg PA
CBHW071304040426
42444CB00009B/1864